One Man's Beliefs

The Theology of Doctor John

By
Dr. John Lawrence

Published by New Generation Publishing in 2013

Copyright © Dr. John Lawrence 2013

First Edition

The author asserts the moral right under the Copyright, Designs and Patents Act 1988 to be identified as the author of this work.

All Rights reserved. No part of this publication may be reproduced, stored in a retrieval system or transmitted, in any form or by any means without the prior consent of the author, nor be otherwise circulated in any form of binding or cover other than that which it is published and without a similar condition being imposed on the subsequent purchaser.

www.newgeneration-publishing.com

 **New Generation Publishing**

Permission to Quote

Scriptures: King James Bible (KJVB)
Scriptures: New American Standard Bible (NASB)

Preface

"The unexamined life is not worth living."
Socrates

I am not a theologian, and do not intend to be. I was predestined to be a Christian and to think like a Methodist. My father's father, John Isaac Lawrence, was a Christian gentleman and responsible for starting Wesley Chapel Methodist Church at Six Mile, Alabama. My father grew up on a farm and was influenced by a Christian father, mother and family. He attended Wesley Chapel Methodist Church on Sunday mornings and Six Mile Baptist Church Sunday school on Sunday afternoons. He left the farm and attended Birmingham Southern College. After graduation he became a Methodist preacher. He left the farm but never lost the love for God's good earth and what it gave us.

My mother was raised under the influence of a Christian father and mother. My mother's father was a carpenter but felt the call to preach and became a preacher in the Alabama Conference of the Methodist Church. My mother's mother was a devout Methodist preacher's wife, and told Mother that if she wanted to be happy in life she should marry a Methodist preacher. Mother sought after and found my father, "farmer Lawrence", and became a Methodist preacher's wife. My father and mother served churches and people in the South Alabama and the North Florida Conference of the Methodist Church.

I ate, slept, ate and breathed Methodist Christian beliefs all of my developing years. Although my father and mother were active in the

Methodist Church, I never heard them find fault with or criticize any other denomination, race, nationality or creed.

When I was a child I thought like a child, spoke like a child and reasoned like a child. As a child, God was a great big man with long, flowing white hair and a long white beard. He had soft, warm eyes and was dressed in a white flowing robe, sitting on a throne made of pure gold. In front of Him was a huge wooden desk, on which was a huge book filled with every person's names and what they had done in life. He would read in the book about my life and what I had done and would decide whether to send me to heaven or hell. That scared the hell out of me.

During my developing years I didn't think much about God except when I went to Sunday school and church. I did believe that I had to be baptized with water, go to church and do the things that Daddy, Mother and my teachers told me to. After high school I entered Huntingdon College in Montgomery, Alabama, to become a Methodist preacher like my father.

When I entered Huntingdon, I joined the ministerial association, took courses in Bible, Christian ethics, read two books, answered some questions by two Methodist preachers, took a test and got my local preacher's license. My first sermon was about God, and I thought that it was good. My second sermon was about love, and I thought that it was very good. The third sermon was about faith. When I got home, I spent the rest of the day thinking about it. I realized that what I had said was what I had read, had been taught and what others had said. There were many things that I had doubts about or could not believe. I considered myself to be a Christian agnostic. I changed my major subjects and thought that I might become a doctor. It didn't feel right for me to tell others what to believe when I was not sure myself.

This book is the evolution of my changing beliefs that have developed as I read the Bible, observed the lives of others as I heard their beliefs and observed their action and relationship with others and God. I questioned and meditated on my life and actions in relationship to others, my mind, soul and body, and my relationship to God and his creations.

I prayed to God to tell me what I should do. I begged, pleaded and cried for God to answer me. I read what Emanuel, God with us, said when he came to Earth. He said that He knew what we needed before we asked. He said that when I prayed, to go in my closet and pray to him in secret. I finally thought that God told me to get off my knees, get off my butt and do some things for Him.

This book is a recording of my thoughts and beliefs as I have developed them over the years. It is not my intention to tell others what to believe or how to live. If the readers have gone through doubts and changes in their beliefs and their relationship to God, others and their lives on this earth, maybe it will be of some help to them in reading the authors effort to develop his beliefs.

Scripture quotations are from the King James Version of the Bible (KJVB) and from the New American Standard Bible (NASB). Factual information came from the encyclopedia Wikipedia, the Catholic Encyclopedia.

Some of the proceeds of this book will go to help fund a perpetual funded charity foundation, "Tend My Flock Foundation".

The Old Testament

Chapter One
God's Creation

In the beginning, God created the heaven and the earth. Genesis1:1 (KJVB). In the beginning was the word and the word was with God and the word was God. John 1:1 (KJVB). "I am Alpha and Omega, the first and the last." Revelation 22:13 (KJVB).

God has no beginning or end. This is difficult for us to understand, since we had a beginning at birth and expect to have an end of our physical existence when we leave the earth at death. The apostle Paul told us in first Corinthians that we would not understand all in this life. He said that we would see as looking into a mirror dimly, but when we are with Go, we will join Him in eternal truth.

In the beginning, God created the heavens and the earth. The earth was formless and darkness was over the surface on the deep and the spirit of God moved across the surface of the waters. Genesis 1:2 (KJVB). According to scientists, there are four things God used to build the universe. These are the proton, the neutron, the neutrino, and the electron. So far, scientists throughout history have discovered about one hundred and eighteen elements composed of these things. These are composed of the proton, the neutron and neutrino in the nucleus and the electrons in orbit around the nucleus, held together by chemical bonding. All matter is composed of these elements in different numbers and arrangements. When anything dies or is destroyed, God uses these elements, through decay or destruction, in creating new things.

God recycles everything. There is abundant evidence that the universe was created by a very large exploding mass. Many scientists have investigated and studied the creation of the universe through this explosion and called it the "big bang theory" of the creation of the universe. God created the sun and its solar system through this big bang. The earth, as stated in Genesis, was void and dark until the gases cooled and separated into solid earth and water. Scientists throughout history have believed that matter could not be created nor destroyed, until Albert Einstein found that a small amount of matter could be converted into a large amount of energy through an atomic explosion. This led the way to develop the atomic and hydrogen bombs.

Sir Isaac Newton discovered God's laws of motion and gravity. The first law of motion stated that an object in motion tended to stay in motion in a straight line unless acted on by an outside force, and an object at rest tended to stay at rest unless acted on by an outside force. These laws explains how all of the solar systems stay in place. The heavenly bodies travel endlessly and are kept in orbit by the force of gravity. We do not realize how fast we are moving, because the earth's atmosphere and objects are moving with us. God's laws never change. God never changes. Therefore, we can know that God is truth and we can depend on His laws to remain constant.

What is God? As a child, I thought of God as a gigantic man, all-powerful and all-knowing. I believed that God watched every move that I made and even knew my thoughts. We refer to God as "Him" or "Father". I cannot understand exactly what God is or what God is like. I do not believe that God is flesh and blood or has a gender. In Genesis, God is referred to as "Spirit". "Thomas said unto Him, "Lord, we do not know whither thou goest; and how do we know the way?" Jesus Christ said to him, "I am the way, the truth and the life; no man comes to the Father but by me"." John 14:5, 6 (KJVB). To me this means that everything that is, everything that is real, and everything that exists, is part of the Spirit of God. Everything that men have discovered about the things of this world and all of God's laws are true and we can trust them to always be true and never change. Daniel Webster defined science as classified or systematized knowledge. We know that those things proved to be true and will never change except for new discoveries. Daniel Webster's definition of science has proved to be true.

God said, "Let there be light", and He separated thelight from the darkness. God separated the water from the land, and there was night and day. God created living things in the waters and on the land slowly, in man's terms, by a process that we now call evolution, slow change and adaptations to the environment over time.

God must have created vegetation in the waters and on the land. After, there was an abundance of plants in the waters. God created fish and other sea creatures to feed on the plants. Some of these sea creatures evolved to breathe in the water with gills and on the land with lungs. After many years these animals migrated all over the earth and adapted to their vegetation, climate and environment. Some animals began to be able to stand upright. There were apes, gorillas, monkeys, chimpanzees and Man.

And the Lord God formed Man out of the dust of the ground, and breathed into his nostril the breath of life; and man became a living soul. Genesis 2:7 (KJVB). So God gave Man a soul. Man is the only animal to have a soul that we know. This separates Man from the lower animals. It has been said that the mind of Man is between the spirit and the soul.

And God said let us make man in our image, after our likeness; and let them have dominion over the fish of the sea, and over the fowl of the air, and over the cattle and over all the earth and over every creeping thing that creepeth upon the earth. So God created man in his *own* image; in the image of God created He him; male and female He created them. Genesis 1:26, 27(KJVB).

It is interesting that God said that He created Man in His image and then said that He created Man in our image. We can't understand everything about God as Paul told us. When God came down in the mind and spirit of Christ Jesus, he told us that God is the truth, the way and the life and that God is love. Everything that is, is God or of God. Everything that Man has learned and discovered to be true is of God. Man has called this "science". Daniel Webster defined science as classified or systematized knowledge. One man cannot understand all truth, so Man divided science into the physical sciences and the biological sciences. Scientist specialized in small segments of these sciences. Everything that Man has learned to be true is of God.

God placed Adam and Eve – "Man" – in the Garden of Eden, and they had everything that they needed to live and to enjoy. Then Man decided to eat of the "tree of knowledge" and learned the knowledge of good and evil. Then God drove them out of the Garden of Eden and told Man that they had to earn their livelihood by the sweat of their brow. This was not a curse but a statement of fact.

No sooner than Adam and Eve had two grown sons, jealousy began. Cain became jealous of Abel, and killed him. Because of this murder Cain was driven out of the family and went to the land of Nod, east of Eden, and found a wife. Adam and Eve could not have been the only humans to have evolved, because Cain found awife in the land of Nod.

Bible scholars have called the first five books of the Bible "the Pentateuch", and believed that God chose Moses to write these books. God ordained Moses to be the author of these books, but Moses was a man. There could be some things that Moses did not fully understand.

Man began to multiply on the earth. People turned from God and became wicked and began to steal, rob and kill. God repented that He had created Man and decided to destroy Man and every living thing on Earth, but Noah found grace in the eyes of the Lord. Genesis 6:8 (KJVB). And God said unto Noah, "The end of all flesh is come to me; for the earth is filled with violence through them, and behold, I will destroy them with the earth. Make thee an ark with gopher wood; rooms shalt thou make in the ark, and shalt pith it within and without with pitch." Genesis 6:13, 14 (KJVB). So Noah built the ark, and when the flood came he took into the ark his sons, their wives and daughters and beast of every king and they survived in the ark until the end of the flood. After the flood, God set his covenant with Noah that He would not destroy the earth with flood again and set his bow in the clouds as a sign of His covenant with Man.

Chapter Two
History of the Hebrews

According to Moses, Abram, later to be called Abraham, was born as a descendant of Noah. And Abram took a wife, Sarai, later to be called Sarah. There was a famine in the land and Abraham took Sarah and went into Egypt because of the famine. And it came to pass when he was come near to enter into Egypt that he said unto Sarah, his wife, "Behold now, I know that thou art a fair woman to look upon. Therefore it shall come to pass, when the Egyptians shall see thee that they shall say, this is his wife, and they will kill me, and they will save thee alive. Say, I pray thee, thou art my sister; that it will be with me for thy sake; and my soul may live because of thee." Genesis 13; 10–12 (KJVB).

So when they came into Egypt, the princes of Pharaoh saw her and commanded before Pharaoh and she was taken into Pharaoh's house. There was a plague in Pharaoh's house because of Sarah, most likely a sexually transmitted disease because she had intercourse with more than one prince.

When Abraham and Sarah returned from Egypt Abraham had many sheep and oxen, men servants, maid servants, she asses and camels. Sarah was unable to have a child, probably because of a sexually transmitted disease she acquired in Egypt. Sarah had her Egyptian maid servant to lay with Abraham and she gave Abraham a son. They called him Ishmael. When Ishmael was about fourteen years old, Sarah gave birth to a son of Abraham, even in their old age. And the child grew, and was weaned: and Abraham made a great feast the same day that Isaac was weaned. And Sarah saw the son of Hagar, the Egyptian, who she had borne unto Abraham. Therefore she said unto Abraham,

"Cast out this bond woman and her son: for the son of this bond woman shall not be hair with my son, even with Isaac." Genesis 21:8 - 10 (KJVB). Because of the greed of Sarah Abraham turned Ishmael and his mother out of the family and gave them bread and water to journey into Egypt. It is difficult to believe that God of truth and love smiled on the greed of Sarah or the willingness of Abraham to turn his own son out of the family because of Sarah's greed.

After Isaac and Ishmael buried their father Abraham, Isaac married Rebekah. Rebekah gave birth to twins, E'sau and Jacob. E'sau was the favorite son of Isaac and Jacob was favored by Rebekah. Because Rebekah favored Jacob, she helped Jacob deceive Isaac and Jacob received the blessing and birthright from his father Isaac. According to Moses, Jacob became the leader of the Hebrews.

Jacob took his wife Rachel and their people and animals and went down to the land of Canaan. Joseph was the younger son of Jacob and Rachel when God changed the name of Jacob to Israel. Then Rachel gave birth to the youngest son of Jacob and named him Benjamin. Joseph's older brothers were jealous of Joseph because he was the favorite son of Jacob. They sold Joseph into slavery into Egypt. Because of Joseph's ability to interpret dreams of the good years and famine in Egypt, he was made lord over the storage of grain and food during the good years to be used during the famine. Following the famine, a new king came into power in Egypt and the children of Israel were made slaves.

The Israelites grew in number and the new Pharaoh believed the Israelites would outnumber the Egyptians and overthrow them. So Pharaoh set taskmasters over the Hebrews and made slaves of them. Pharaoh had the midwives kill every Hebrew baby boy.

Moses was born to the wife of one of Joseph's descendents and the midwife did not kill Moses. Moses's mother hid him in a basket in the edge of the Nile. When an Egyptian princess found Moses, she took him to live in the palace of Pharaoh and found a nursemaid to nurse Moses, who was Moses's mother.

When Moses became a man, he killed an Egyptian who was mistreating an Israelite. He fled into the desert and lived there for a while, until God spoke to him and instructed him to return to Egypt and tell the Pharaoh to let the Israelites go. After some magic tricks, the Israelites fled and crossed the Red Sea. It is difficult for me to believe that God resorted to magic tricks and plagues to make the Egyptians let the Children of Israel go free. But that was the way Moses told it.

After the Israelites crossed the Red Sea and were free, they wandered in the wilderness until they grew in number. The Israelites wanted to have a god that would lead them into battle against their enemies. They made a golden calf as a god to lead them. Moses destroyed the golden calf and eventually brought them the commandments that God gave him. These commandments were ten as follows.

"I am the Lord thy God which has brought you out of the land of Egypt, out of the house of bondage.

Thou shalt have no other god before me.

Thou shalt not make unto thee any graven image, or any thing of any likeness of anything that is in the heavens above, or that is in the earth beneath, or that is in the waters beneath the earth.

Thou shalt not take the name of the Lord thy God in vain.

Remember the Sabbath day, to keep it holy.

Honor thy father and thy mother: that thy days may be long upon the land which the Lord thy God giveth you.

Thou salt not kill.

Thou shalt not commit adultery.

Thou shalt not steal.

Thou shalt not bear false witness against thy neighbor.

Thou shalt not covet thy neighbor's house. Thou shalt not covet thy neighbor's wife, nor his manservant, nor his maidservant, nor his ox, nor his ass, nor anything that is thy neighbor's."

Exodus 20:2–17 (KJVB).

After Moses gave the Israelites the "Ten Commandments", the children of Israel lived in the land and grew in number. Moses gave the Israelites instructions in how to build an ark of the covenant and what to put in it. He also gave them instructions in how to build an altar, upon which to offer sacrifices to God. It is difficult for me to believe that God wanted things to be burned in order to worship Him. God has been the Spirit of Love and Truth. From the beginning, God does not need nor have a desire for burnt offerings. The Israelites were young in the understanding of God and wanted something they could see and feel to worship. To them God was with them and would lead them into battle against their enemies.

Joshua led the Children of Israel by the Red Sea over to the River Jordan past the children of E'sau. "But Si'hon, King of Hesh'bon, would not let us pass by him: for the Lord thy God had hardened his spirit and made his heart obstinate, that he might deliver him into thy hand, as appeareth this day. And the Lord said to me, "Behold I have given Si'hon and his land before thee; begin to possess, that thou mayest begin to inherit his land. Then Si'hon came out against us, he and all his people, to fight at Ja'has. And the Lord our God delivered him before us; and we smote him and his sons, and all his people. And we took all his cities at that time, and utterly destroyed the men, and the women, and the little ones, of every city. We left none to remain". Deuteronomy 2:31–34 (KJVB). It does not make sense; it does not compute. I cannot reconcile the fact that God told the Children of Israel, *"Thou shalt not kill"*, and before their life was over tell them to kill all men, women and children. I cannot believe that the God of love and truth would tell us not to kill, murder, at one time and then tell us to murder those that He has created.

According to Moses, God told the Hebrews to destroy other nations, cities, and even burn their orchards and all of their idols. God told Moses that He was a jealous god. Since God is the beginning and the end and creator of all things, including all mankind, I cannot believe that He could be jealous of anything. Moses thought that God was the god of the Children of Israel and would lead them in battle to kill all others. This I cannot believe either. When Christ, Emanuel, God with us, came to Earth, he told something different. Moses instructed the Hebrews in the commandments of God, what sacrifices to make on the altar, laws and statutes that pertained to the Hebrews only. The Hebrew nation became very legalistic. They were told what they could and could not eat and what they could and could not do on the Sabbath.

After the death of Moses, God came to Joshua, saying, "Moses, my servant is dead; now therefore arise, go over the Jordan, thou and all the people, unto the land which I do give to them, even to the Children of Israel. Every place that the sole of your foot shall tread upon, that have I given unto you, as I said unto Moses." Joshua 1:2, 3 (KJVB).

Joshua did as he believed the Lord had told him. Joshua led the Children across the river Jordan. The priest carried the "Ark of the Lord" before them and blew their trumpets and the men shouted loud and the walls of Jericho fell down and the men killed every man, woman, little one, sheep, donkeys and everything in the city. According to Joshua, God told him what to do. The Israelites have been warring people ever since. That is not the God that I believe in.

And the Lord said unto Joshua, "Fear not, neither be thou dismayed: take all the people of war with thee, and arise, go up to A'ia: See. I have given into thy hand the King of A'ia and his people, and his city, and his land: And thou shalt do to A'ia and her king as thou didst unto Jericho and her king: only the spoils therefore and the cattle thereof shall ye take for a pray unto yourselves: lay thee an ambush for the city behind it." Joshua 8: 1, 2 (KVB)

The Lord god of Israel acted as a general and planned the battle to slaughter all the people of A'ia and her King.

I cannot believe that this was the God that came to earth in the Christ to show the Israelites and all of us how to live in love for each other and how to live in peace and to forgive and to do good to those who trespass against us. I cannot believe that God changes, otherwise we could not trust His word.

After Joshua destroyed A'ia, the people of the next city had heard what Joshua had done and as the Israelites approached they pleaded with Joshua and asked him not to slaughter them but make them servants to the Children of Israel. Joshua made them hewer of wood and drawers of water and took them with him. Joshua believed that the Lord God of Israel wanted to lead them in battle. Joshua led the warriors of the Children of Israel against many people and cities and destroyed them. He took their silver, gold and livestock as his own. I cannot believe that the God of truth and love told Joshua to destroy the people of His creation.

Now after the death of Joshua it came to pass that the Children of Israel asked the Lord, saying, "Who shall go up for us against the Canaanites first, to fight against them? And the Lord said, Judah shall go up: I have delivered the land into his hands". Judges 1:1, 2 (KJVB). Judah led them in battle until they came to Jerusalem. They fought against Jerusalem, slaughtered the people and burned the city. The Children of Israel fought against many cities and killed many people, led by judges and military leaders. They would turn away from God, worship false gods and they would be killed. After they repented, the Lord God of Israel would choose leaders, lead them into battle, slaughtering people and taking their land, cattle, silver and gold as spoils of war. To the Children of Israel God was a war god who would lead them in battle against their enemies and anyone whose land and possessions they desired. I believe that they knew no better, and disobeyed many Commandments that God had Moses give them, such as "thou shall not kill, thou shall not covet, thou shall not commit adultery, and thou shall not worship any other god".

Samson was a Hebrew. He is described as a powerful, strong man, made strong by God through the hair of his head. He killed many Philistines until he finally told a harlot, Delilah, the secret of his strength. While she had him asleep she cut his hair off, then the Philistines bound him and threw him in prison. While Samson was tied to the pillars of a large hall, he prayed for God to give him his strength back. According to the Old Testament, Samson regained his strength, pulled the pillars and killed all of the people in the great hall. It is difficult for me to believe that the God of love and truth would do that.

Ruth

The book of Ruth is believed to have been written by the prophet Samuel.

In the days of the judges there was a famine in the land. A man of Bethlehem went into the land of Moab with his two sons and his wife Naomi. The sons took wives in Moab. One of the son's wife was Ruth. Naomi's husband and both sons died. Naomi heard that the famine had ended and decided to return to her land and her family. Naomi told her daughters-in-law to return to their mother's house. Ruth told Naomi that she was her son's wife and would stay with her and care for her. Ruth said, "Do not urge me to leave you or turn back from following you; for where you go I will go and where you lodge I will lodge. Your people shall be my people and your God my God." Ruth 1:16 (NASB).

Naomi and Ruth returned to her kinsmen near the city of Bethlehem. A kinsman of Naomi's husband Boaz came to them and let them gather grain in his fields. Boaz found favor with Naomi and Ruth and gave them threshed grain. Boaz instructed the young men not to molest Ruth. Boaz took Ruth to be his wife and Ruth gave him a son, Obed. Obed's son was Jesse and Jesse's son was David.

First Samuel

First Samuel is believed to have been written by Samuel and the prophets Gad and Nathan.

"And this man went up out of his city to worship and sacrifice unto the Lore of Host in Shiloh: And the two sons of Eli, Hopniand and Phinehas, the priests of the Lord, were there". I Samuel 1:3 (KJVB). I cannot believe the God who created the earth, man and everything on the earth could wish for man to sacrifice animals in order to worship and please Him, as pagans do. I do not believe that the God who created the entire universe needs us to praise him in that way. The God of love and truth commanded us to take care of his creation and help those who are in need.

And this man had two wives. One of his wives was Hannah, who was barren and had no children. Hannah prayed to God that He let her have a son. She promised God that if He let her have a son she would give him to the Lord. The son was born and Hannah named him Samuel. After Samuel was weaned, she took him to the house of the Lord and gave him to Eli. When Samuel was young he had a dream that someone called him and he went to Eli and said, "Here I am". After the third time Eli said that it was the Lord and to say to Him, "Lord, here I am". So Samuel served Eli and the Lord until Eli died and then he was the prophet of God for Israel.

The Children of Israel turned from God and began to worship Baal. The Philistines had slain many Israelites and had taken the Ark of the Lord. According to Samuel, the Philistines were slain because of the Ark of the Lord and they returned the Ark. Samuel spoke to the people and they returned to the Lord of Israel. God chose Saul and Samuel anointed Saul to be King of the Children of Israel. Samuel said unto Saul, "The Lord sent me to anoint thee to be king over his people. Over Israel; now therefore hearken thou unto the voice of the words of the Lore." I Samuel 1:1 (KJVB).

Saul was king of Israel for years, and slew many of their enemies. Saul fell out of favor with the God of Israel because of things that he had done and not done. God chose David, the shepherd boy, the son of Jesse, to replace Saul. The Philistines came to battle Israel with a giant. David told Saul of his ability to kill lions and bears in defense of the sheep. He stood before the Philistine giant and killed him with a stone from his sling. He took the sword of the giant and cut the giant's head off and took the head to Saul. "And it came to pass as they came, when David was returned form from the slaughter of the Philistines, the women came from all cities of Israel, singing and dancing, to meet King Saul, with tabrets, with joy, and with instruments of musick. And the women answered one another as they played. And said, "Saul has slain his thousands, and David his ten thousands". 1 Samuel 8:6, 7 (KJB). Saul continued to be king but became afraid and jealous of David and tried to kill him or have him killed. David fled and when Saul followed him to have him killed, David had several occasions on which he could have killed or had Saul killed but he would not destroy Saul. The Philistines fought the people of Israel and slaughtered them. They killed Saul's two sons. Saul fell on his own sword and took his own life. The people at that time believed that each nation had a god of its own that would lead them in battle against their enemies. There were constant slaughter of men and sacrifice of animals. The people of that time could not believe and understand that God was the creator of all things and had the desire for all man to live in harmony, love and brotherhood.

Second Samuel

Second Samuel is believed to have been written by Samuel and the prophet's prophets, Gad and Nathan.

Saul and David continued to fight and slaughter the Philistines and other enemies. Saul and his men became weakened against the Philistines and Saul asked his arm bearer to kill him but the arm bearer would not. So

Saul took a sword and fell on it and died. David was grieved of Saul's death but some of the sons and followers of Saul continued to fight against David. Finally David became king of the Children of Israel and built a great city of Jerusalem.

David had concubines and wives and had many children. One day David saw a woman washing herself and had her brought to him. She lay with him and conceived. Her name was Bathsheba, the wife of Uriah. King David had Uriah sent to the front of a battle and Uriah was killed. God was displeased with David because of this. David broke three of the Commandments of God; "thou shall not kill, thou shall not covet and thou shall not commit adultery". However, King David continued to build a great city of Jerusalem and a great nation. I believe that the people at that time had an immature understanding of what God was. The early Hebrews as well as other people believed that there was a god of each people that was a war god that would lead them in battle against their enemies and a god that would help them gain land to live in, wealth, and worldly possessions.

King David and the Children of Israel continued to war against their enemies. Absalom, one of the sons of David, and some of the Israelites desired to make Absalom King of Israel. King David and his followers fled from Jerusalem. When Absalom led his followers to find and fight the followers of David his long hair became entangled in the limbs of and oak tree. Some of the servants of David found Absalom and killed him. David restored the Children to worship the Lord God of Israel.

First Kings

It is believed by some Bible scholars that First Kings was written by Jeremiah and some of the prophets.

King David had his son Solomon anointer King of Israel and Judah after his death. King Solomon had the men that were against his father, King David, killed and he did great things in Israel and Judah. He built a great house in Jerusalem in which to worship God. He used a lot of gold, silver cedar and stone to build the temple. He made icons of angles and lions and moved the ark of the God of Israel into it. His throne was overlaid with gold. He made friends with Egypt and took an Egyptian to be one of his wives. Solomon developed a navy and traded for gold, silver lumber and spices with other nations and the queen of Sheba. Solomon began to make friends with women of other nations and began to worship their gods. The followers of King David had the kingdom of Israel and Judah removed from Solomon.

Sons of the house of David and sons of the house of Solomon became kings over Jerusalem, Judah and other tribes of Israel. There were prophets and other "men of God" who rose up and helped to decide who would be the leaders of the tribes of Israel. When Solomon died he was buried in Jerusalem. After Solomon's death the king of Egypt came to Jerusalem and took away all the treasures out of the King's house and all of the shields of gold.

The tribes of Israel continued to fight and to change kings. The King of Syria sent messages to the tribes of Israel demanding gold, silver, their wives and children, but the Israelites fought against the Syrians and defeated them.

Ahab, the king of Israel, demanded the vineyard of Naboth but Naboth refused. Jezebel, the wife of Ahab sent a letter to Naboth demanding the vineyards and sent men accusing him of blaspheming God and the king and they took Naboth out and stoned him to death. So the Children of Israel continued to fight and slay each other in order to gain control of Israel and Judah and gain things for themselves. Many continued to worship other gods. The early people of Israel and Judah continued to believe that their god would be a war god who would protect them from their enemies and provide for them.

Second Kings

Many biblical scholars believe that Second Kings was written by Jeremiah.

According to the words of Elisha: "And he went up from thence to Bethel: and as he was going up by the way, there came forty little children out of the city, and mocked them, and said unto him, go up thou bald head; go up thou bald head. And he turned back and looked upon them, and cursed them in the name of the Lord. And there came forth two she-bears and tare forty two children of them". 2 Kings 2:23, (KJVB) I cannot believe that the God of love and truth would cause this to happen to little children that He loved.

According to Jeremiah, Moab rebelled against Israel after the death of Ahab. Ahaziah, the king, became ill and turned to Baalzebub, the god of Ekron to heal him. The Lord God of Israel sent and angel to the prophet Elijah and told him to tell King Ahaziah to return to the Lord God of Israel or he would surely die. The king sent three groups of fifty men to bring Elijah to him. Elijah would not, so the Lord God of Israel sent fire from heaven and consumed the men. So Ahaziah died according to the word of the Lord God of Israel.

The king of Syria took his men and chariots and camped around Israel. When Elisha heard this he prayed to the Lord to make the Syrians blind, and the Lord did. Elisha led them to Samaria. Then Elisha prayed to the Lord to let the Syrians see and He did. When they could see they invaded Samaria instead of Israel.

King Ahab, his sons and followers had turned fromthe Lord God of Israel and worshiped Baal. Alisha had Jehu anointed King of Israel. King Jehu had Jezebel, who had helped destroy some of the prophets of the Lord, thrown down and killed. Jehu had his men slay the sons and followers of King Ahab. Jehu had the people that followed Baal to gather to sacrifice and worship Baal, to gather in their place of sacrifice and worship. Then he had all of them killed. Jehu thought that he had cleared all the followers of Baal removed from Israel. When Jehu died, his son, Jehoahaz, reigned in his stead.

The people of Israel turned from the Lord and beganto worship Baal again. Syria overran Israel and oppressed the people. The kings of Israel, Judah and Samaria, battled each other for several years. The king of Israel and the king of Judah tore down part of the wall of Jerusalem and took the gold, silver and precious things to the house of the Lord.

The people of Jerusalem and Judah had many kings. Some of them were very young. They fought back and forth. Few tried to turn again to worship the Lord God of Israel. Mostly they began to worship Baal and other gods. The King of Babylon, Nebuchadnezza, destroyed Jerusalem and Judah.

Chronicles

It is believed that the book of Chronicles was written by one man, probably a Levite, and later edited by Hebrew theologians.

The books of first and second Chronicles are the early Hebrew's recording of the history of the Children of Israel from the time of Joshua to the capture of Israel and Judah by the Persians.

Ezra

Ezra was first written on scrolls by scribes and Hebrew theologians and was called Ezra-Nehemiah, later to be divided into two books, Ezra and Nehemiah.

The children of Israel were taken into captivity and taken to Babylon. The treasures of the temple in Jerusalem were taken to the treasure house in Babylon. Cyrus, the king of Persia, believed that God wanted the House of the Lord to be rebuilt in Jerusalem. All the tribes of Israel were returned to Judah and they re-built the House of the Lord and returned all the treasures.

Ezra prayed long prayers to God concerning the sins of the people that had been taken into captivity. Many of the men of captive Hebrews had taken wives of the people of other lands. Ezra called all the elders, the priest and Levites together and discussed the matter. They decided to separate the strange wives and their children from the Hebrew nation. Mixed marriages to people of other lands were not allowed, keeping the Hebrews a pure people.

Nehemiah

It is believed that Nehemiah was written by scribes that wrote Ezra, and was first Ezra-Nehemiah and then divided into two books, Ezra and Nehemiah.

While the Hebrews were exiled, Nehemiah prayed to the Lord God of Israel and believed that God wanted him to return to

Jerusalem and rebuild the city of Jerusalem. At that time he was cup-bearer to the king of Persia. King Artaxerxes sent him back to

Jerusalem with materials to rebuild the walls, gates and House of the Lord. Other nations did not believe that he could and began to fight against him. Nehemiah set guards while the workers rebuilt the walls, gates and the House of the Lord. The scribes and priest recorded the history of the Hebrews and the people began to worship the Lord and record the Commandments and laws of God.

Nehemiah had the people of Israel to clean themselves. He organized the priests, the Levis, the singers, the keepers of the treasures, and the prophets. Those who did not keep the Commandments and the law were turned out of Jerusalem. Those of mixed marriages and the children of mixed marriages were not allowed to live with the people of Jerusalem. Only pure Jews could live with each other.

Esther

The book of Esther is believed to have been written in the third or fourth century B.C. by Mordecai, the uncle of Esther. Some believe that it was a historical novel based on the conditions of the times.

Esther was a Jewish girl whose father and mother had died. She was raised by her cousin Mordecai who was a devout Jew. The king of Persia requested his queen to come before the princes in his presence because she was beautiful and good to be looked upon. The queen refused and the king became angry. The king then instructed his servants to bring to him the most beautiful virgins in the land. One that they found and brought to him was Esther, the cousin of Mordecai, the Jew. The king selected Esther to be his queen.

A man named Hamon became angry with Mordecai because he would not bow down to him and the king. Hamon persuaded the king to turn to him and have him kill all the Jews. Hamon built a tower to hang Mordecai on. The king found out that Mordecai was the one that notified him of two men that plotted to kill him and wanted to reward him. Because of Esther and Mordecai the king canceled the orders to exterminate the Jews and hanged Hamon instead.

Through the efforts of Esther and Mordecai the slaughter of many Jews was prevented. The Lord God of Israel was never mentioned.

Job

No one knows who wrote the book of Job. It isbelieved to have been written as a poem and later changed into a narrative story. Some pages are found in the Dead Sea scrolls and in Egypt.

As the story goes, Job was a man who believed in, trusted and worshiped God. Job was a mm of wealth. He had three sons, two daughters and many servants. He had many sheep, cattle, asses and oxen. During a feast God and Satan observed. And Satan said that he could make Job turn from God. Fire came from heaven and consumed Job's animals and his servants. Then fire consumed Job's children. Job cried, rent his clothes, poured ashes on his head but prayed to God and burned sin offerings to God. Then Satan caused sores and boils to cover Job's skin. Still Job would not turn from God even though his friends pleaded with him to curse God and die.

Job prayed to God and praised Him to all the people. He continually told of how great God was and what God had done. God told the three friends of Job to go to Job and have him pray for them. They returned to Job, who prayed to God for them. Then God returned everything that Job had lost and more. He had many cattle, sheep, horses and camels. Job's skin was healed and Job had seven sons and their daughters. Job lived a hundred and forty years, enjoyed a good life and died in old age.

The Psalms

The book of Psalms was written by David, the son of Jesse. The Psalms were written to praise Yahweh, the Great King. The psalms were played before King Saul and for worship services in the temple and for weddings.

David, son of Jesse, wrote the Psalms while he was tending the flocks by himself and when he played and sang before King Saul. Most of the Psalms were about the relationship of the early Hebrews, the dangers they faced and their belief in the Lord God of Israel. The twenty-third Psalm is an example of David's request of God, for His help in times of trouble and to obtaining land and things that he needed, wanted and his defense against his enemies.

"The Lord is my shepherd; I shall not want. He maketh me to lie down in green pastures: he leadeth me by the still waters. He restoreth my soul; he leadeth me in the paths of righteousness for his name's sake. Yea, though I walk through the valley of the shadow of death, I will fear no evil for thou art with me; thy rod and thy staff they comfort me. Thou preparest a table before me in the presence of mine enemies: thou anointest my head with oil; my cup runneth over. Surely goodness and mercy shall follow me all the days of my life: and I will dwell in the house of the Lord for ever." Psalms 23:1- 6 (KJVB).

David was striving to understand God and how to worship Him. Psalm 100 is an example: "Make a joyful noise unto the Lord all ye lands. Serve the Lord with gladness: come before his presence with singing. Know that the Lord He is God: it is he that hath made us, and not we ourselves; we are his people and the sheep of his pasture. Enter into his gates with thanksgiving; and into his courts with praise: be thankful unto him, and bless his name. For the Lord is good; his mercy is everlasting; and his truth endureth to all generations." Psalm 100 (KJVB).

The Proverbs

Most Bible scholars believe that the Book of Proverbs was written by Solomon. Some believed that parts of Proverbs was either written by or transcribed by Hezekiah.

The statements in Proverbs seem to be an effort to obtain wisdom and knowledge of God and His laws and Commandments. Some of the proverbs were concerning righteousness, which was understanding and obeying God's Commandments as given to the Children by Moses. Those who obeyed God's laws would have a long and prosperous life. Emphasis was placed on "Thou shalt not lie, bear false witness against thy neighbor, honor thy father and thy mother, not becoming drunk and not to steal and not to takeadvantage of the people with unfair lending practice." There was emphasis on teaching children the Commandments of God and to love the Lord and to take care of the poor.

Ecclesiastes

Ecclesiastes is believed to have been written by Solomon in his old age, reflecting on the meaning of life and death and refers to himself as Koholeth, which meant "preacher" or "teacher".

The words of the preacher, the son of David, king in Jerusalem. "Vanity of vanities, saith the preacher, vanity of vanities; all is vanity. What profit hath a man of all his labor which he taketh under the sun? One generation passeth away and another generation cometh: but the earth abides forever." Ecclesiastes1:1-4 (KJVB).

Solomon reflected on his life and attempted to gain wisdom and knowledge of God and the meaning of life under the sun, life on earth and taught and preached this to the people. He taught that life under God and his commandments gave Man joy and pleasure on the earth. He taught that God gave us everything that we needed by his sun and rain to grow the food and things that Man needed. Solomon desired to have his wealth and power but taught that he and people should take care of those in need.

"Rejoice, O young man, in thy youth; and let thy heart cheer thee in the days of thy youth, and walk in the ways of thine heart, and in the sight of thine eyes; but knoweth thou, for all these God will bring thee into judgment. Therefore remove sorrow from thy heart. And put away evil from thy flesh: for childhood and youth are vanity." Ecclesiastes 11:9- 10 (KJVB Solomon reflected on his youth and attempted the youth to walk not in evil but in the ways of God.

The Songs of Solomon

Most scholars attribute the authorship of the Songs of Solomon to King Solomon.

King Solomon wrote the songs about himself and the things that he had. He was proud of his power and possessions and loved the bodies of women. King Solomon had seven hundred wives and three hundred concubines. Some of his songs were about what women thought of him and what they did to him. This is evident in the following verses: "Who is this that cometh out of the wilderness like pillars of smoke, perfumed with myrrh and frankincense with all powder of merchants? Behold his bed, which is Solomon's; threescore men are about it, the valiant of Israel. They all hold swords, being experts in war: every man had his sword upon his thigh because of fear of the night." Songs of Solomon 3:6 - 9 (KJVB).

Solomon was vain, as he had discussed earlier abut young men. Solomon loved the bodies of women; he did not mention the name of any or his wives. He tells us of what he thought of the body of women in the following verses: "How beautiful are thy feet with shoes, O prince's daughter! The joints of thy thighs are like jewels, the work of the hands of a Cumming workman. Thy navel is like a round goblet which wanteth no liquor: thy belly is like heaps of wheat set about with lilies. Thy two breasts are like two roes that are twins. Thy neck is like a tower of ivory; thy eyes are like the fish pools of Heshbon: thy nose is as the tower of Lebanon which looketh toward Damascus. Thy head upon thee is like Carmel, and the hair of thine head like purple; the king is held in the galleries. How pleasant and fair art thou, O love for delight!" Songs of Solomon 7:1 - 6 (KJVB). Solomon was self-centered and broke the commandments of coveting and adultery.

Isaiah

It is believed that chapters 1 - 39 were written by the prophet Isaiah. Chapters 40 - 55 were written by an unknown author in Babylon. Chapters 56 - 66 were written by an unknown after the return of the Hebrews to Israel after the fall of Babylon.

"To what purpose is the multitude of you sacrifices unto me? Saith the Lord: I am full of burnt offerings of rams, and the fat of fed beast; and I delight not in the blood of bullocks, or of lambs or of goats." Isaiah 1:2 (KJVB). The prophet Isaiah had begun to understand what God was like and what He desired. He stated that God did not wish that the things that he created be burned as offerings to Him.

Isaiah spoke of the sins and wickedness of the people and the destruction of the people by wickedness and evil. He did predict the coming of a Messiah. "For unto us a child is born, unto us a son is giver: and the government shall be upon His shoulders: and His name shall be called wonderful, Counselor, The mighty God, The everlasting Father, The Prince of Peace. Of the increase of his government and peace there shall be no end, upon the throne of David, and upon His kingdom, to order it, and to establish it with judgment and with justice from henceforth even forever. The zeal of the Lord of hosts will perform this". Isaiah 9:6, 7 (KJVB).

Isaiah prophesied to King Hezekiah that God would return the people of Israel from Babylon to Jerusalem and that King Hezekiah would die. King Hezekiah turned to God and was given fifteen more years to live until his sons killed him.

The rest of the book of Isaiah was concerning the people who tried to understand good and what He could do for them. They tried to understand God's wrath, his forgiveness and how He would help them survive. They believed that he would send water to the desert and land for them to grow trees, vineyards and plants for food. They began to believe that God would bring peace to the people.

Jeremiah

The book of Jeremiah is believed to have been written by the prophet Jeremiah.

Jeremiah believed that he was a prophet of God. He believed that God told him that He would cause the people to be captured and taken into Babylon for many years. Jeremiah believed that he communicated with the Lord God of Israel and prophesied the things that God would do. He told the people how the wrath of God would destroy kings, people and nations because of their evil ways and their worship of other Gods. Jeremiah wore a yoke about his neck and preached in the streets that God's anger was against them because of their evil ways and disobedience.

Finally Jeremiah prophesied that the Lord God of Israel would return the people from Babylon if they turned back to the Lord God of Israel. I cannot believe that the God of truth and love would destroy or punish anyone. I believe that God created the earth and the laws that govern the earth and all living things. It is for us to learn and understand these truths and laws, and when we do we may live a long peaceful life.

Ezekiel

Ezekiel was written by Ezekiel, who had a vision at age of thirty and believed that he was chosen to be a prophet of God.

At age thirty Ezekiel had a vision. In the vision he saw a chariot coming in a whirlwind, driven by four living creatures like men with four faces, one like a man, one like a lion, one like an oxen, and one like an eagle.

Each had four wings. The chariot was on wheels, one wheel within the other and had eyes. It came to him like the rushing of water. The spirit of God spoke to Ezekiel and told him that he was a prophet and he was to speak to the people of Israel and tell them to turn from their evil way and return to worship the Lord God of Israel. Those that did not hear him and did not return to Him, He would require their blood and they would die. Those who listened to him would live.

Daniel

It is believed that the book of Daniel was written by the prophet Daniel during the second century B.C.

Daniel was a prophet. When King Nebuchadnezzar invaded Jerusalem and took the children of Israel into captivity in Babylon Daniel had many dreams and visions. King Nebuchadnezzar had a dream that he could not understand and none of his people couldinterpret it for him. He was going to have them killed. Daniel was brought to the king and interpreted the dream for him. King Nebuchadnezzar had created an image of gold and silver and mud and required all people to bow down and worship it. Three friends of Daniel's; Shadrach, Meshach and Abednego refused to worship the king's image. King Nebuchadnezzar had them thrown into a fiery furnace. They were seen walking around with the image of another man. When they came out they were not burned.

When King Darius was king, he decreed that all should worship him and his god. Daniel refused and continued to worship and pray to his God. King Darius had Daniel thrown into the den of lions. The following morning Daniel was in the den and the lions had not bothered him and he told King Darius that the angle of his God had protected him. King Darius then began to worship the God of Daniel. The rest of the book contained the visions and dreams of Daniel.

Hosea

The book of Hosea is a collection of the prophet Hosea during the eighth century B.C.

Hosea claimed to be a prophet of God. He spoke of all of the evils of the Children of Israel. Sometimes Hosea wrote as though he was a prophet; sometimes he wrote as though he was God. He wrote of all the evil things the people were doing. The nation was whoring. The young women were whoring to obtain something to eat and drink. The wives were committing adultery. The people were lying, stealing, killing and worshiping other gods and idols. Hosea wrote of the anger of God and how God would persecute them, dry up their springs, dry the land and the trees would die and there would be nothing to eat. He wrote of how God wanted to forgive them and restore them to a good life.

Hosea tried to understand God and to gain knowledge. He began to realize that God desired justice, mercy and love for others. As other prophets he tried to gain knowledge of God and God's will for man.

Joel

The book of Joel was written by the prophet Joel, one of the minor prophets, one of the twelve in about the year 400 B.C.

Joel writes about the plague of locusts that destroyed the crops, vineyards and the pastures of Judah. There was no rain and the rivers and land dried up. Joel urged the Children of Israel to return to the Lord their God. He told them to fast, dress in sack clothes and cry to

God. He told the priest to cry and howl to the Lord and praise Him only. Then Joel told the Children of Israel how the Lord would send the rain and sun and restore the vineyards and pastures. He urged the fighting men to fight the gentiles and return the sons and daughters to Judah and Jerusalem.

As like the other prophets, Joel believed that everything that happened to the Children of Israel came about because the people had turned from the Lord and his Commandments and began to worship other gods.

Amos

Amos was one of the first prophets and wrote the book of Amos.

Amos was a herdsman and felt that God called him to prophecy to the people of Judah and Jerusalem. He wrote to them of the things that God would do to them because they had turned from Him. They had been liars, selfish, had not taken care of the poor and had turned from the Commandments. Amos wrote to them of the things that God would do to them. Many would be hungry, thirsty and be taken into captivity and many would die by the sword. God would not receive their sacrifices, destroy their temples and houses and land. Amos wrote that God would restore the house of David and Jacob if they would return to the Lord.

Jonah

It is not understood who wrote the book of Jonah. Some believe that the book was written by Jonah. Some believe that it was written by others and compiled into the book.

According to Jonah the Lord appeared to him and told him to go to the big city of Nineveh and cry to them for they had been a wicked city. Jonah was frightened and boarded a ship to run away from God. God caused a great wind and a storm and the ship wasin danger. Jonah was cast into the sea and the storm ceased. God prepared a great fish, which swallowed Jonah and vomited him on the shore of Nineveh.

When Jonah came to Nineveh he cried to the people and they dressed in sack clothes and begged for forgiveness. The people prepared a booth for Jonah to speak from. It was hot, so God grew a great gourd, which gave shade to Johan. When the sun came up again God sent a worm to eat the gourd. God finally asked Jonah whether he would spare Nineveh, a city of sixteen thousand people, or not. The answer was not given in the book.

I cannot believe the God spoke directly to Jonah and told him to cry to the city. I cannot believe that God caused a great storm or a great fish. I believe that God's laws do not change and I do not believe that God created a great fish especially to swallow Jonah and vomit him on dry land. Jonah would have drowned, suffocated or been destroyed by a fish's digestive acids and enzymes.

Micah

The book of Micah was written by the prophet Micah during the seventh century B.C.

Micah, like the rest of the prophets, wrote to the people of the judgment of God and the sins and the wickedness of the people of Israel. He wrote of the way God would punish them for their iniquities and what God would do for them if they returned to the Lord. Micah began to understand what God desired to give to the people if they would turn to Him. He began to understand what God wanted of Man.

Micah wrote to the people what he believed the Lord required of them. As he said, "Wherewith shall I come before the Lord and bow myself before the high God? Shall I come before Him with burnt offerings, with calves of a year old? Will the Lord be pleased with thousands of rams, or with ten thousand rivers of oil? Shall I give my firstborn for my transgressions, the fruit of my body for the sins of my soul? He hath shewed thee, O man , what is good; and what doth the Lord require of thee but to do justly, to love mercy and to walk humbly with thy God." Micah 6:6 - 8 (KJB).

Nahum

The book of Nahum was written by the prophet Nahum, probably in Jerusalem in the seventh century B.C.

Nahum tried to understand God. He wrote that God was a jealous god. He wrote that God loved forgiveness and mercy but hated those who did not worship Him and were not righteous. Nahum described God as mighty and could tear down mountains, break the rocks to pieces and dry the rivers and seas. The people were sinful, full of lies, violence and whoredom. God would utterly destroy the wicked. His anger was great and his revenge was strong. He would destroy nations and the children would be torn to pieces in the streets. I believe that Nahum had a vivid imagination and was influenced by the other prophets. Man did not understand God until He came to Earth in the mind and spirit of Christ.

Habakkuk

The book of Habakkuk was written by the prophet Habakkuk in the seventh century B.C.

Habakkuk believed that he was having a conversation with the Lord. He asked how long he would have to cry to Him for Him to answer Him. The Chaldeans were marching through the land.

He told God that the people were lying and stealing and crying to other gods. Habakkuk talked to God as though God was coming down to destroy the land until the people returned to Him. Habakkuk wrote of God returning prosperity to the people and giving salvation to them if they would return to Him.

Zephaniah

Zephaniah wrote the book of Zephaniah during the days when King Josiah was king of Judah.

Again Zephaniah writes for the wrath and anger of God for the wickedness of the people. He tells how God will destroy the unfaithful. Then Zephaniah writes how God will drive out the enemies and return the people that return to Him and build them a great nation.

Haggai

The book of Haggai was written by the prophet Haggai in about 528 B.C., that was shortly after the Hebrews returned to Jerusalem after a long captivity in Babylon.

The prophet Haggai wrote of his conversations with the Lord God. The Lord told him to speak to the king of Judah and the high priest and tell them that it was time to rebuild the temple in Jerusalem. The Lord said that he would destroy their enemies and help them rebuild the temple if they would worship him and work to rebuild the temple.

The New Testament

Chapter Three
The Book of Matthew

There are some arguments about who wrote the Gospel according to Matthew. Most believe that Matthew wrote his gospel.

Matthew tells of a man named Joseph who was a descendant of King David who was betrothed to a lady named Mary. Joseph discovered that Mary was with child and planned to put her away privately, but an angel appeared to Joseph in a dream and told him that the child was conceived by the Holy Spirit and the child would be named Emanuel, which was interpreted as "God with us".

There were three wise men who heard that a messiah would be born and they began to search for Him. King Herod heard this and told the wise men to let him know where the child was. A star appeared to the wise man and they followed it to Bethlehem. They worshiped Him, left gifts and went to their country away from King Herod. An angel appeared to Joseph and told him to take Jesus into Egypt where they stayed until the death of King Herod.

John the Baptist began to preach of the coming of Jesus and began to baptize his followers with water. When Jesus was baptized by John, the heavens opened and the Holy Spirit descended upon Jesus the Christ.

Jesus went up into the wilderness to fast and to pray and to prepare for His ministry. The devil tempted Jesus three times. The devil took Jesus to the pinnacle of the temple and told Him to throw himself down. Jesus would not because He knew that God's laws could not be broken and if He fell to the street He would be hurt or killed. He knew that it was not the time nor the place.

When Jesus came down, He walked by the Sea of Galilee and saw two men, Peter and Andrew, fishing. He told them to follow Him and He would make them fishers of men. They left and followed Jesus and became His disciples. Jesus saw two men mending their nets, James and John, and told them to follow Him. They left their nets and followed Jesus.

Jesus began teaching in the streets and in the synagogues and where people were. He began to perform miracles and to heal the lame and the sick. Soon large crowds were following Him. Jesus led them into the mountain where he gave the "sermon on the mount". Matthew wrote the words of Jesus the Christ, Emanuel, God with us, as he heard Christ. These were the words of God.

As Christ taught them, He said, "Do not store up for yourselves treasures on earth, where moth and rust destroy, and where thieves break in and steal. But store up for yourselves treasures in heaven where neither moth nor dust destroy and where thieves do not break in and steal; for where your treasure is, there your heart will be also." Matthew 6:19 - 21 (NASB).

Large crowds followed Jesus, listening to his teaching and asking to be cleaned and healed. Christ healed the sick and afflicted, cast out demons and raised the dead. Christ took the disciples into the mountain by themselves to teach them. He asked them who the Son of Man was. Some said that He was John the Baptist. Some said that He was Elijah or one of the prophets. He said to them, "But who do you say that I am?" Simon Peter answered and said, "You are the Christ, the Son of the living God." And Jesus said to him, "Blessed are you, Simon Barjona, because flesh and blood did not reveal this to you, but my Father who is in heaven. I also say to you that you are Peter, and upon this rock will I build my church; and the gates of

Hades will not overpower it." Matthew 16:15 - 18 (NASB).

Jesus continued to teach and preach, and large crowds followed him. Christ rode into Jerusalem on Palm Sunday with large crowds sing and praising Him. He entered the temple and drove the merchants and money-changers out because they were defiling the house of prayer. Children came to him and the disciples tried to stop them, but Christ said for them to let thechildren come to him for of such is the kingdom of heaven. He told the disciples that unless their faith was not as a little child they should not enter the kingdom. He told them not to store up treasures but to share with the poor and that it was difficult for a rich man to enter the kingdom of heaven. I do believe that God wishes for us to care for those who are in need.

Christ was teaching the disciples and told them of the end of time, the coming of the Son of Man and of Judgment day and said, "The king will say to those on His right, Come you who are blessed of my father, inherit the kingdom prepared for you from the foundation of the world. For I was hungry, and you gave me something to eat; I was thirsty and you gave me something to drink; I was a stranger and you invited me in; naked and you clothed me; I was sick, and you visited me; I was in prison and you came to me." Then the righteous answered Him: "Lord, when did we see the hungry and feed You, or thirsty and gave You something to drink? And when did we see You a stranger, and invite you in, and naked and clothed You? When did we see You sick, or in prison, and came to You?" The King will answer and say to them, "Truly I say to you, to the extent that you did it to one of the least of these brothers of mine, even the least of them, you did it to me." Matthew 25:34 - 40 (NASB).

When the Passover feast was to be observed, Jesus had the disciples to gather with him to have the last supper. After supper he went to the Garden of Gethsemane to pray. Judas came with the priest and a crowd, kissed Jesus and betrayed Him. The synagogue leaders had false witnesses testify against Jesus. They beat Him with their fists and spat on Him. They took Him to Pilot and demanded that he be crucified. They tortured Jesus and the soldiers beat Him, mocked Him and nailed Him to a cross. A man named Joseph had the body of Jesus prepared and laid in his tomb. On the third day, Mary Magdalene and the other Mary found the tomb empty. Angels told them that Jesus had risen and they worshiped Him. He appeared to the eleven disciples and they worshiped Him.

I believe that Matthew wrote of the life of Jesus as well as he remembered and understood. I believe that what he quoted of what Jesus spoke were the words of God.

The Gospel of Thomas

The Gospel of Thomas was written by the apostle Thomas.

Thomas wrote of Jesus as the other apostles did. He understood and used different words, but what he said that he heard from Jesus were the words of God. He wrote the greedy and selfish being unable to see the kingdom of heaven.

The Gospel of Peter

It is believed that the apostle Peter wrote the Gospel of Peter.

Peter wrote about the trial, crucifixion and resurrection of Christ. Peter's account was the same as

Matthew and Thomas. Peter did not write of the sayings of Jesus.

The Gospel of James

The Gospel of James was written by James, the brother of Jesus.

James was the brother of Jesus. James wrote about a woman and a man who had no children but were loyal in the Israelite faith.

The woman prayed long for the Lord to let her have a child. She finally conceived and gave birth to a female child. That child was dedicated by the Hebrew church leaders. That child was named Mary and she became Mary the mother of Jesus. James wrote about her birth and the reactions of King Herod and the three wise men. I believe that James did his part in the preparation of the coming of Jesus, the Christ, Emanuel, God with us.

The Gospel of Mary

It is believed that the Gospel of Mary was written by Mary Magdalene.

Mary was a close follower of Jesus. She was at the crucifixion of Jesus and one of the first to be at the tomb and found that Christ had risen. Mary had dreams of talking with Christ and told the disciples of these dreams. Some of the disciples did not believe that God or Christ would appear to and rely on a woman. Peter said to them that Mary was the most beloved woman of the savior. Then Mary told them of her dreams and visions. Jesus said that there was no sin in the world but that the sins were in the minds of man. Mary told them of one of the conversations. And she began to speak to them these words: "I", she said, "I saw the Lord in a vision and I said to Him, "Lord, I saw you today in a vision. He answered me and said to me," "blessed are you that you did not waver at the sight of me. For whoever the mind is there is the treasure". I said to Him," how does he who sees the vision see it, through the soul or through the spirit?" The savior answered and said, "He does not see through the soul nor through the spirit, but the mind that is between the two. That is what sees the vision is". Mary 7:8 - 11.

The Gospel of Philip

The Gospel of Philip was written by the apostle Philip.

Philip tried to understand the creation of the world and Man. He wrote that Christ was the Son of God. He wrote that those who believed in Christ were Christians and those who did not remained a Hebrew. Philip wrote that the Holy Spirit was a gift and those that received it would believe that truth and love were gifts of the Holy Spirit. He wrote that Christ was crucified in order for us to believe and enter the kingdom of God.

The Gospel of Mark

The author of the Gospel of Mark is not really known. Most scholars believe that the gospel was written by Mark, mostly from translation of the preaching of Peter. Some scholars believe that part of the gospel was added as late as the second century.

Mark wrote of the things that Matthew did in his gospel. He told of John the Baptist preaching of the coming of Christ for the redemption of sin. He told of the baptism of Jesus and of the descent of the Holy Spirit on Jesus and the forty days that Jesus spent in the wilderness being tempted by the devil. Mark told of how Jesus taught and healed the sick, and how He made the leper clean. Jesus drove demons out of some people and healed the lame. The word of what Jesus was doing spread to many people and great crowds followed Him.

Mark wrote of many things that Jesus said and things that Peter told him that Jesus said. He wrote of Jesus casting out demons, healing the sick and lame, restoring sight to the blind and raising the dead. Mark told of the last supper, the garden where Jesus prayed and was taken into custody. He told of the trial, the crucifixion and reappearance of Christ. I believe that what Mark wrote were the words of God, spoken by Christ, Emanuel.

The Gospel of Luke

The Gospel of Luke was written by the apostle Luke.

The apostle Luke writes of the same things that happened while Jesus was with them as did Matthew and Mark. He wrote of the disciples traveling with Jesus, healing, teaching, casting out demons and raising the dead. People were amazed and large crowds followed them. The priest and other synagogue leaders were worried that Jesus would take their kingdom from them. They were constantly trying to find something wrong with Him and have Him killed.

And He looked up and saw the rich putting their gifts in the treasury. And He saw a poor widow putting in two small copper coins. And He said, "Truly I say to you this poor widow put in more than all of them; for they out of their surplus put into the offering; but she out of her poverty put in all that she had to live on". And while they were talking about the temple, that it was adorned with beautiful stones and votive gifts, He said, "as for those things which you are looking at, the day will come in which there will not be left one stone upon another that will not be torn down." Luke 21:1 - 6 (NASB).

The Gospel of John

It is not known for sure who wrote the Gospel of John, but most Bible scholars believe that it was the Apostle John.

"In the beginning was the word, and the word was with God and the word was God. He was in the beginning with God. All things came into being through Him, and apart from Him nothing came into being that has come into being. In Him was life, and the life was the light of men." John 1:1 - 4 (NASB).

The apostle John wrote of the miracles that Jesus had performed, healing the sick, restoring sight, healing the crippleand raising the dead. Jesus had done these things so that the people would believe that He had the power of God. Jesus was mocked, tortured and crucified on the demand of the Hebrew religious leaders and some of the Hebrew people. Jesus was dead and buried and placed in a tomb. On the third day Christ appeared to them in different places, even in a closed building with the doors shut. I believe that Christ was a spirit. I do not believe that the earthly body of Jesus could have appeared in so many places and could have entered though closed doors and walls. I do believe that his words were the words of Jesus Christ, Emanuel, "God with us". They were the words of God.

The Book of Acts

It is believed that Luke wrote the Book of Acts.

Luke wrote that after Christ ascended to heaven the apostles were together and discussing what they were to do. The Holy Spirit descended on them and they were filled with the spirit of God. They began teaching, preaching and healing the sick and lame. The synagogue leaders and the orthodox Hebrews began to persecute, stone and kill those who preached and taught in the name of Jesus Christ.

One of the devout believers of Christ and taught in His name was Stephen. One of the believers in the old Hebrew religion was a man called Saul. He led in the suppression of the new believers in Jesus Christ, the Son of God. He led the people in the persecution, imprisonment and stoning to death of the new believers and approved of the stoning of Stephen. Saul thought that he was doing the will of God.

On the road to Damascus Saul was blinded and Jesus Christ appeared to him in a vision and asked him why he was persecuting Him. After a few days the Holy Spirit came to him and his sight was restored. His name was changed to Paul and he began to travel to cities by land and ship as far as Rome. Paul was beaten, arrested and thrown into jails. The synagogue leaders in Jerusalem tried to have him killed but he was carried to Rome to be tried before the Roman courts and was finally released.

I do believe that God did influence the followers of Christ and the miracles of healing and visions. This I believe was necessary for the spread of the word of God and His truth and love to people around the world. I believe that Luke wrote the best that he could the word of God.

The Book of Romans

The Book of Romans was written by the apostle Paul to those in Rome who were believers in Christ.

After the conversion of Saul he was named Paul and was a devout believer in Christ. Paul began to preach the word of God to the Hebrew people and returned to Jerusalem. Because of his preaching and teaching in Jerusalem, the priests and synagogue leaders had him arrested and put in jail. The Romans would not have him killed and sent him to Rome.

Paul travelled by foot and by ship and preached the gospel of Christ, the Son of God, to everyone that he could on the way. In

Rome there were many converted to the Christian way of belief. The Jews and Gentiles argued over the law. Paul tried to teach them to love one another even if their beliefs were different. Paul traveled over the coast of the Mediterranean Sea and preached and taught and helped establish churches in many cities.

Paul struggled in his beliefs but said that different beliefs of the law were not that important if we lived the life of the love of God through Christ Jesus.

First Corinthians

The Book of First Corinthians is an epistle written by the apostle Paul to the people of the church of Corinth.

The apostle Paul wrote this epistle to the church in Corinth to encourage them and to instruct them in the way they should worship God and how they should treat each other including those of other nationalities and belief. Paul tried to teach them what they should do and was still quite legalistic. He tried to understand life and death. Paul tried to teach them of the relationship between men and women. He stated that men were responsible to God and women were responsible to men. He preached about marriage, adultery and sex between two men.

Paul did come to some good conclusions before he finished the epistle. Paul wrote, "Love never fails; but if there are gifts of prophesy, they will be done away, if there are tongues, they will cease; if there be knowledge, it shall be done away. For we know in part and prophesy in part; but when the perfect comes the partial will be done away. When I was a chil, I spoke like a child. thought like a child, reasoned like a child; when I became a man I did away with childish things. For now we see in a mirror dimly, but then face to face; now I know in part, but then I will know fully just as I have been fully known. But now faith, hope, love, abide these three; but the greatest of these is love." 1 Corinthians 13:8 - 13 (NASB).

Second Corinthians

The Book of Second Corinthians was written to the people of the church of Corinth.

The apostle Paul wrote this letter to the people of the church in Corinth to encourage them to remain faithful to his teachings and the teachings of Christ. Paul pleaded with them not to have discord but to love and respect each other. Paul boasted that he had not cost them or taken anything from them. He stressed to them to love one another and to give their gifts to those in need. He warned them of false prophets and false teachings. He thanked them for receiving Titus whom he had sent to them. He boasted that he was humble and that what he was telling them was from God. He promised to come to see them for the third time.

Galatians

The Book of Galatians was written to the people of the church in Galatia.

The apostle Paul continued to spread the word of God through Jesus Christ to as much of the Gentile world as he could. He wrote of his beliefs that the Hebrew people were all descendents of Abraham and lived under the law of Abraham and Moses. Paul taught that Isaac was born to a free woman and should have inherited everything from Abraham. He wrote that the son of the bond slave, Hagar, was not free and should not have inherited anything of Abrahams. I believe that this was an error in his thinking.

Paul wrote that circumcision was of the Hebrew law and was not necessary to live in the spirit of Christ and inherit eternal life. Paul did write of the wrongs of greed, selfishness, anger and hatred. He did write that people should live in peace, love for each other and giving freely to the poor and those in need. He did believe that we should live in the spirit of Christ and not by the old laws.

Ephesians

The Book of Ephesians was written by the apostle Paul to the people of the church in Ephesus to encourage them in the faith.

The apostle Paul wrote to the people of the church of Ephesus that he was commanded by the Lord Jesus Christ to them and to other Gentiles. Paul believed that Christ had converted him to spread the gospel to the Gentiles. He wrote the people of the church of Ephesus of the love of God and encouraged them to love one another, to avoid anger, hate, greed and being dishonest to their fellow men. He wrote to them to love their wives, their servants and to spread the words of Jesus Christ through the way that they lived. He tried to understand God, heaven and the eternal life. He encouraged the Gentiles to do the same.

Philippians

The Book of Philippians was written to the people of the church in Philippi.

The apostle Paul continues to spread the message of Christ to the Gentiles. He boasted of the way the people of Philippi had received the spirit of truth and love and had turned to worship Christ Jesus. Again Paul stressed the importance of living in the

Spirit of God and not in the flesh. He boasted to the Philippians of the way they had lived in the spirit and helped and gave to those who were in need. They were taught by Paul of the importance of living by the spirit more than the law. Paul thanked them for what they had sent him and helped his missionary journey but toldthem that he did not need any more economic help. Paul tried to live and preach in such a way that he would live in the kingdom of God with Christ Jesus.

Colossians

The apostle Paul wrote Colossians to the people of the church in Colossae.

Paul wrote to the people of Colossae to praise them and to encourage them to love one another and to spread the word of Christ Jesus and the kingdom of God. Paul thought of the kingdom as a place where Christ would be sitting by God. He stressed prayers for others and to praise God. He encouraged them and himself of the prize we would receive when we got to the kingdom of God.

First Thessalonians

The apostle Paul wrote these words to the Thessalonians.

The apostle Paul wrote to the Thessalonians to praise them for the work they were doing to spread the message of Christ and the kingdom of God. He asked them to pray unceasingly and hold steadfast in their beliefs. He stressed the glory of salvation in the Lord to those who remained faithful to God and destruction to those who did not.

Second Thessalonians

Second Thessalonians was written by the apostle Paul to the Thessalonians.

Paul wrote the Thessalonians praising them for their steadfast faith in the Lord Jesus Christ and their help in spreading the gospel. Paul seemed to believe that Jesus Christ was coming back with His host of angels to destroy those who did not believe and practiced sinful ways. He wrote to the people to try to get the unbelievers to believe and to work. Those who did not work were not to be fed. Paul praised them for their brotherhood, charity and for their work to spread the gospel of the Lord Jesus Christ.

First Timothy

The Book of First Timothy was written to Timothy by the apostle Paul.

The apostle Paul wrote this book to Timothy to instruct him in the way he should live and what he should teach. He urged Timothy to live a godly life and to teach and act in truth, love and to teach men the truth of Christ Jesus but not to judge them or argue with them. Paul instructed him to always be a good example to others.

Paul taught against selfishness, greed and to avoid the love of money. He encouraged Timothy to teach the rich to share their wealth with others and to take care of widows and poor. Paul believed Christ would return before their death and take them with him into the kingdom of heaven. Paul was a strong teacher in doctrine. He urged Timothy to do the same.

Second Timothy

The gospel of Second Timothy was written by the apostle Paul, Paul wrote to Timothy to praise him and to encourage him. Paul told Timothy of the Persecutions and the time that he was imprisoned because of his preaching and teaching and that God through Christ Jesus had sustained him. Paul instructed Timothy not to get in arguments with those with lies, greed, love of money, earthly things, lust and desire to be in high places. He updated Timothy on the others who were workers for the spread of the gospel.

Titus

Paul wrote this book to Titus in Crete.

The apostle Paul wrote this book to encourage and to instruct Titus in Crete. He wrote that he should not argue with those of a different doctrine. He wrote that he should be an example to everyone by the way that he lived and by what he said. He instructed Titus to teach the women to be faithful to their husbands and to their children. Paul encouraged Titus to live a godly life,abstaining from arguments, desires for self-gain and to avoid too much wine. Again Paul spoke of the return of Christ Jesus to take them to the kingdom of heaven.

Philemon

Paul wrote the book of Philemon to Philemon and his family.

Philemon had become a believer in Christ Jesus and a fellow worker in spreading the joy and peace of Christ to his family and those around them. Paul sent them greetings from himself and Timothy. He told them that he thanked God for him and his family and that he prayed for them every day.

Hebrews

No one really knows who wrote the book of Hebrews. Many people have been suggested, but there is no agreement as to the author.

The writer of Hebrews reflected a lot on the old Hebrew history back to Abel, Noah, Abraham, Jacob, Moses and Joshua. The author wrote as though Jesus was a high priest and the messiah was to be a military leader. The author wrote of the sacrifices of animals and blood to God. The blood of Jesus was believed to be a blood sacrifice to God for the redemption of man and to make a new covenant with God. I cannot believe that the author had a good understanding of why Jesus died and what Christ was all about.

The Letter of James

It is believed that the letter of James was written by James, the brother of Jesus.

James wrote to the twelve tribes scattered abroad, teaching them and encouraging them to have faith and believe in God and Christ Jesus. He wrote of being honest, avoiding being boastful and ministering to the needs of others. He encouraged them to avoid earthly possessions for themselves but to give what they had to the poor widows, orphans and those who are in need. He encouraged them to avoid being boastful and not to try to be in the high places and not to appear better than others.

First Peter

The gospel of Peter was written to the people scattered through the Hebrew world and Asia.

Peter wrote to the new believers to encourage them to be steadfast in the faith. He stressed the love and the fellowship with others and to let themselves be a good examples to others. He preached that in order to earn eternal glory and peace with God we may need to suffer as Jesus Christ did. But he encouraged them to be honorable and upright and by doing so we would go with Christ to glory when he came back.

Second Peter

Simon Peter wrote this to the new believers.

Simon Peter wrote to encourage the new believers to be steadfast in the faith of God and Jesus Christ. He warned them of false teachings and to avoid the wicked ways of unrighteousness, lust, greed, adultery and sinful ways of the flesh. Peter told them of the new heaven and the new earth and that the old earth would be destroyed by fire and the unrighteous would be destroyed. He wrote of the return of Christ who would take the believers to the new glorious heaven with him.

The First Letter of John

The first letter of John was written to those who believed in God and his son, Jesus Christ.

The Apostle John wrote to the new believers of the love and truth of God, and that God so loved the world that he sent his only son to the world to give us the spirit of love and truth and to save us of our sins. John stressed that we should love God and our neighbor as ourselves and not the world. He stressed that Christ Jesus was coming again to take those who loved God and their fellow men with him away from the earth and the evil ones into the kingdom of heaven and eternal life.

Second John

The second epistle of the apostle John was written to the lady and her children, which is believed to have meant the church and believers.

The apostle John wrote these words to the church and the believers. John warned them of other false doctrines and that those who had different doctrines and were not of the same beliefs. Those were the antichrist. John instructed the believers not to let these people into their house. However, he stressed the doctrine of love and truth as had been spoken of by Jesus Christ many times.

Third John

The apostle John wrote the book of Third John.

The apostle John wrote to Gaius, who traveled with the apostle Paul. He warned him of men who thought that they were more important than others and wanted to have the first place in the church. One man had even turned some out of the church if they did not agree with them. John stressed truth and love and that all people were important to God. We have some people like that today.

The Letter of Jude

The epistle of Jude was written by Jude, the brother of James. No one knows which James he was a brother of.

Jude wrote the epistle to the believers in Christ. He refers a lot to the Old Testament and the judgment of God and the destruction of the unbelievers. That is about all that Jude stressed in this short epistle.

Revelations

The book of Revelations was written by the apostle John.

The apostle John wrote the book of Revelations as a book of prophesy to the believers in God and Christ Jesus. John felt as though this book was the final word to the believers in Christ. John had a dream or a vision. In this vision God was dressed in white cloth with gold on the clothes. God was sitting on a throne and had a book of life. God was surrounded by servants and angels. There were living creatures with different heads, horns and tails. The angels were there to help God punish the wicked and to help destroy the world. The seven angels had bowls of gold and would pour out things to help destroy the sinful world. Those who were marked for salvation and eternal life would be with God and Christ in the New Jerusalem. Those who were wicked, liars, murders, and those who lusted after the flesh would be thrown into a lake of fire and brimstone.

Summary

God knew that the early Hebrews had become legalistic and came to the earth in the spirit of truth and love to tell the people how they should live together. Jesus was born of the Virgin Mary and was named Christ, Emanuel, which is interpreted as "God with us". King Herod and the synagogue leaders did not desire to lose their power and planned to kill Jesus. After thirty years they did succede in killing Jesus.

Jesus was baptized by John the Baptist, and the Holy Spirit, the spirit of truth and love, descended on Him. Jesus was tempted by the devil but would not yield to him. The devil tried to get Jesus to jump from the top of the temple but Jesus would not because He knew that God's laws were not to be broken and that He might be broken or killed. Jesus knew that that was not the time or the place.

Jesus preformed miracles, healed the lame, healed the sick, drove out demons and raised the dead. I believe that Christ did these things so that the people would believe in Him. Jesus Christ taught them in His sermon on the mount. He said, "Blessed are the peace makers for they will be called the children of God." He said, "Blessed are the poor for they shall inherit the earth." He taught them not to be greedy and not to store up treasures on Earth but in Heaven.

The disciples ask Jesus what the judgment day would be like. Christ told them that they took strangers in, fed the hungry, clothed the naked and came to those who were sick and those who were in prison. Christ said that these would be with God in the Kingdom of Heaven forever. Those who were selfish and self-centered and did none of these things would be in outer darkness.

Christ asked the disciples who he was. Simon Peter said to Christ, "Thou art the Christ, the Son of the living God." Christ told Peter that he was correct, that he was God and Peter was Peter and upon that rock He would build His church.

Mary Magdalene told the disciples that she had a vision of Christ. Christ told her that there was no sin in the world but that the sins were in the minds of Man and that the treasure was in the mind. Mary asked Christ how she saw visions, through the spirit or through the soul. Christ told her that she saw visions in the mind and that the mind was between the spirit and the soul.

Jesus was asked where he was going. Jesus answered and said, "I am the way, the truth and the way. No one will see the Father except by me. I and the Father are one."

In the book of Acts of the Apostles, Luke wrote of the Holy Spirit coming to the apostles and causing them to speak in tongues so that they could preach and teach in the language of the people they were speaking to. Luke also wrote of the apostles as they witnessed and taught of the words of Christ. He also tells of the conversion of Saul and renamed Paul. Paul was devout in his spreading the word of God and Christ Jesus as he was against the believers before his conversion.

The apostle Paul began to teach and preach the gospel of Christ in Jerusalem, but the synagogue leader had him arrested and tried to have the Romans kill Him. The Romans would not kill Paul and sent him to Rome to be tried before Caesar. Caesar released him and Paul taught the word to many churches and people except in Asia. The other apostles taught and preached the love and truth of God and Christ. They still held to the Hebrew history and the doctrines and Commandments given by Moses. They were despised and jailed by many as non-believers. Many listened to them and the churches were established. They stressed the love and truth of God as taught by Christ. They taught of love and help to their fellow men and women. They did teach and believe that Christ would return for them and take them to the Kingdom of Heaven.

My Beliefs

When I was born my mind was blank. I knew nothing, but did have instincts. I could cry when I was hungry, cold, or hurt. I was born into a Methodist minister's home and family. As I watched and listened, I began to think and believe as a Christian. When I was young, I believed that God was a very large and strong man. He sat behind a very large desk with a great book, "The Book of Life". I did not know how it got there, but God could look in that book and see everything that I had done. I thought that when I died and went before God, He would read from the Book of Life and decide whether I was to be sent to Heaven or Hell. I did not want to go to Hell in a lake of fire and burning brimstone. When I entered college, I was planning to be a Methodist preacher like my father. I studied, listened to teachers, preachers, read and obtained my local preacher's license. My first sermon was about God and I thought that it was good. My second sermon was about love and I thought that it was very good. Some ladies told me that it was the best sermon and that if I did not make a preacher I would miss my calling. I felt good and that gave me the "big head". The third sermon was about faith. When I returned to my room at school I thought very hard and decided that I had regurgitated what I had heard and read and that I did not believe a lot of what I had said. The next semester I changed my major and became a pediatrician.

Christ did tell us to bring up a child in the way he should go and in his old age he or she would not depart from it.

People have tried to understand the origin of the earth and the meaning of life since the beginning of time. I believe in one God, the creator of the universe and everything in it. I have been taught to call God "God" and "Heavenly Father". Other people have called God by different names and have thought of God in different ways and what God expects of Man.

The ancient Greeks believed in more than one God. They tried to understand the origin of the world and Man. Some of their gods they created in their literature, poems, art and plays. They believed in a god of the earth, a god of the sea, a god of fertility, a god of love, and a god of war. For a time they believed that some of the gods existed along with mortals.

The first five books of the Old Testament were written by Moses. Some people proclaim that God dictated the entire Bible. This I cannot believe. I do believe that God did have something to do with Moses, as he wrote the books. I believe that the account of the creation was true.

The people did become greedy, lustful and wicked, and God did destroy at least part of the world by flood. Then Noah started a new civilization.

Abraham did become the leader of the Hebrew people. I do not believe that God was pleased by the greed of Sarah causing Abraham to turn Ishmael out of the family. I wonder what history would have been like if Ishmael had remained in the family.

I cannot believe that God told Joshua to murder every man, woman and infant in Jericho and the other villages on the way to the "Promised Land". God had just given the Ten Commandments to Moses and said that you should not murder or covet. Yet Joshua killed every living thing and took the gold, silver and best livestock and a spoil of war.

I cannot believe that God desired the children of Israel to burn animals as a sacrifice to God. Micah did see some things that he believed God desired. God did not desire rivers of oil or many sheep. He had set the laws to create them. Micah said that God did not require the life of their first born for the redemption of Man's sins. Micah stated that all God desired of Man was to do justly, love mercy and walk humbly with Him.

Joshua traveled across Canaan and slaughtered every one that he came to, except one group that pleaded with him to make them servants, so Joshua took them with him and made them hewers of wood and drawers of water. All of the judges and kings after Joshua believed that the Lord God of Israel was their god only and if they worshiped Him He would lead them into battle and help them destroy their enemies.

The people in and around Israel and Judea worshiped a god called Baal. Some believed that Baal was the god of rain and fertility. Others believed that Baal was the god of unity of the family, the father and the strength of the mother who kept the family together. Some of the Israelites began to worship and built temples to Baal. One of the kings worshiped Baal and married a daughter of a non-Israelite.

The Children of Israel believed that the Lord God Israel was a war god and led them in battles to slay their enemies. They believed that the Lord God of Israel would not help them if the did not worship Him and obey the Commandments of God. Some of them believed that to worship God they should build Him a temple, make vessels of gold and cover the ark and altar with gold and cover the throne with gold and silver icons.

The early Hebrews believed that they were the chosen people of God. God came down in the spirit and mind of Christ to try to teach them the way to live in peace, joy and love for each other. Because of their beliefs of the Hebrew king, and religious leaders that the Messiah was to be a military leader they killed Jesus by hanging Him on a cross.

God came to earth in the spirit of Christ, Emanuel, God with us. He came to teach us how to live in peace, joy and love for each other. I believe that accounts of the actions that occurred were as accurate as the apostles knew how. I believe that when they quoted the things that Christ said they were the words of God.

Christ taught us to love one another and our neighbor as ourselves. He taught us to share and help those in need. He rebuked those who were greedy and tried to store up wealth on earth. The rich ruler would not give up his possessions to follow Christ. The farmer that built for himself larger barns to store what he had grown died before he could use them. The religious leaders killed Jesus because they did not want to give up their high places of authority. God said, "Blessed are the meek."

Jesus was scourged, beaten and hung on a cross to die. One of the thieves recognized Jesus as the Christ and said that He had done no wrong. He asked Christ to remember him when He got to His kingdom. Christ said to him, "This day you will be with me in Paradise". On the third day the tomb was empty. I do not know what happened to the physical body of Jesus. Christ rose from the tomb and appeared to people in different places. The spirit of Christ, Emanuel, appeared to the believers gathered in a closed building. It had to be the spirit because a physical body of flesh, skin and bone could not have gone through walls and closed doors. It had to be the spirit of Christ that ascended into heaven because a physical body rising would havedefied God's laws of gravity. Many people worship the cross because they say that Christ died to wash away our sins. This is like pagans think. Some think that the blood of Jesus washes away their sins and they can do as many sinful things as they wish and they will be washed away by the death and blood of Jesus. I cannot believe this. The instructions of Christ were simple: truth and love for God's creations and love for our neighbor as ourselves.

The apostles and other believers began to spread the word of God to the Gentiles and the people of Asia. They taught the gospel of truth and love. They continued to think in the way the Hebrews thought. They were legalistic and taught the laws and Commandments of Moses. They did begin to believe in the teachings of Christ. They believed that Christ would come back for them in this life and take them to heaven. Christ had taught that the kingdom of Heaven, the kingdom of love and truth was at hand now.

The apostle John had dreams and visions of the end of time. He had dreams of God on his throne with angels pouring out things from golden bowls to destroy parts of the earth and seas. He had visions of animals with multiple heads and feet roaming the earth. He described Hell as a place of fire and brimstone where those that were not "saved" would be cast into at the end of their life. Christ told the disciples the righteous would be with God and the unrighteous would be cast in outer darkness. I do not believe that God would inflict pain and suffering on anyone. I believe that those who believe in God and live in the spirit of love and truth and as Christ taught will be in the warmth of God's love for eternity. There have been many beliefs about God, man and creation of the world and everything in it. The early Hebrews believed that they were the chosen people of God and that God, the Lord God of Israel, promised them life and the promised land. It was alright to kill innocent people in order to gain the land. They believed that they must obey the Commandments given to them by God through Moses. Today there are many different Jewish beliefs among Jewish people around the world.

There are many anti-Semitic feelings and beliefs throughout the world. The people in the land of Syria, the lands around Israel, Egypt, the mid-east, and Europe have anti-Semitic beliefs. Some Germans developed strong anti-Semitic feelings during the Holocaust when Hitler and the Nazis believed that the Aryan people were the chosen people and tried to exterminate the Jews. It would be great if people could disagree without being disagreeable, but that will probably never be.

Some of the more recent Jews and Christians have tried to be more tolerant of others beliefs and practices. Some even intermarry and live in peace.

The Muslim religion was started by Muhammad. Muhammad secluded himself in a cave when he was forty years old. He fasted and said that he had visions that God spoke to him and told him that he was a prophet. Muhammad said that God instructed him to write the book, the Quran. From this writing he started the Muslim religion, which is a monotheistic religion. Muslims believe that God, which is called Allah in their language, was the God of Abraham, Noah and Moses. They believe that Jesus was mortal and the last great prophet until Muhammad.

Their religion is Islam, which means "submission" and to make peace. They believed in charity, tolerance of other religions, many rituals and prayers. They believe in pilgrimages to Mecca and had battles over the control of Mecca. Muhammad tried to have peace and cooperation with other people. As with other religions, there are sects that have other beliefs. Many Muslims, Jews and Christians have been slaughtered by some of these sects. Islamic *jihad* is believed by some factions of Muslims to be the way to destroy the infidels that oppose Islam and those Muslims that do not believe as they do. They believe that their ultimate goal is to establish Islam as the only religion in the world, and that those who are killed in a *jihad* are guaranteed an immediate entry to paradise without torment of the grave. They will immediately receive seventy-two beautiful maidens as wives.

The Hindu religions are the oldest religions dating back to prehistoric times. There are many different beliefs among the Hindu. Some believe in Hinduism as a religion and some believe it is a "way of life". Some of them have built large beautiful temples to worship in and sing chants and to pray much as the Jews, Muslims and Christians. Some Hindus believe in truth and love, about the same as Christ taught. Some do not believe in a god. Most believe in a god but none state that they completely know what God is, similar to what the apostle Paul wrote. Most believe in peace, truth, love and respect for those who beliefs are different. Many believed that God is a great soul and Man's soul is what will exist forever. They did have some wars but not as many as the Hebrews, Muslims and Christians. Many did not believe in revenge and to have respect for others as well as all of God's creation.

Buddhism has been described as a religion. Others have thought that Buddhism to be a way of life. There are many beliefs and practices among Buddhist. The underlying practices of Buddhism are meditation and self-purification. Buddhism places importance on truth, respect of others and charity. Some believe in death and others believe in rebirth. They have temples and ceremonies, as do most religions.

When the pilgrims landed at Plymouth, they were greeted by friendly Native Americans. The Pilgrims were strangers and the natives welcomed them in. They were hungry and the natives helped feed them. The pilgrims and the Indians developed trading and fur trapping. When Myles Standish lured two natives into his place and stabbed them to death that stopped the friendly relations between the two.

The Iroquois Nation was the largest group of Native Americans in the Northeastern North American continent. They had fertile soil for crops, a large quantity of wild game and many fish. They believed that the Great Spirit cared for the sky, earth, water and every living creature. They believed in caring for others and the earth. They believed that when they left this life their soul would go to join the Great Spirit. The Puritans came in the name of Christianity, and believed that they were the chosen people of God. They had no problem in driving the native Iroquois from their homeland so that they could have it to live in. I cannot believe that this was the will of God.

The Dakota or Sioux Indian religion tied them to the land and their existence. They were closely related to the Buffalo and they did not try to separate the real from the unreal. They were in constant movement to stay with the Buffalo, their main source of livelihood.

I believe that there is one God, creator of the universe and everything in it. I believe that all men are created equal and the will of God is for everyone to have a healthy happy life on the Earth. I believe in Christ, Emanuel, "God with us". I believe that God came to Earth in the mind and spirit of Christ to show and to teach Man how to live in peace, love and good will to all men and women. I believe that the greed and desire for power of religious leaders and some of the people had Jesus tortured and hanged on a cross, an emblem of suffering and shame. I believe that Christ appeared on the third day, spoke to and instructed the disciples and others in spreading the gospel of love and truth. I believe that the spirit of God ascended to heaven. I believe in the Holy Spirit, the Spirit of God, the spirit of truth and love. I believe that when we leave this Earth our soul will be with God and in the warmth of His love for eternity.

In summary, all that God requires of Man is to love everyone, mankind, our neighbor, God and ourselves.

May the spirit of love and truth abide in you now and forever.

www.ingramcontent.com/pod-product-compliance
Lightning Source LLC
LaVergne TN
LVHW041549070426
835507LV00011B/1013